To order additional copies of this book, contact:
Xlibris Corporation
1-888-795-4274
www.Xlibris.com
Orders@Xlibris.com

Periodic Table of the Elements

H																	He
Li	Be											B	C	N	O	F	Ne
Na	Mg											Al	Si	P	S	Cl	Ar
K	Ca	Sc	Ti	V	Cr	Mn	Fe	Co	Ni	Cu	Zn	Ga	Ge	As	Se	Br	Kr
Rb	Sr	Y	Zr	Nb	Mo	Tc	Ru	Rh	Pd	Ag	Cd	In	Sn	Sb	Te	I	Xe
Cs	Ba	La-Lu	Hf	Ta	W	Re	Os	Ir	Pt	Au	Hg	Tl	Pb	Bi	Po	At	Rn
Fr	Ra	Ac-Lr	Rf	Db	Sg	Bh	Hs	Mt	Ds	Rg	Cn	Uut	Uuq	Uup	Uuh	Uus	Uuo

La	Ce	Pr	Nd	Pm	Sm	Eu	Gd	Tb	Dy	Ho	Er	Tm	Yb	Lu
Ac	Th	Pa	U	Np	Pu	Am	Cm	Bk	Cf	Es	Fm	Md	No	Lr

INTRODUCTION

The periodic table of the elements is an elegant collection of scientific knowledge. This book will assist the reader in memorizing the essential information presented in the periodic table. Just as the alphabet is basic information in learning the English language, so is the periodic table basic information in understanding chemistry; and chemistry is "elemental" to the study of all science. Everything on earth is made of these elements.

I have divided the table into sixteen sections. Each section of symbols and names can be memorized like a vocabulary list. Use the familiar pictures and words to help recall the information and complete the table from memory. Use the blank table on the back cover of the book to keep track of your progress.

Whether you are a serious science student preparing for a class or an armchair scientist looking for a challenge, you will be surprised at how easy it will be to memorize the table. I hope you will also be surprised at how useful this knowledge will be in understanding science news and literature. Learn this valuable information now and use it for a lifetime.

About the Author:

Eric Fontaine is a native of New Hampshire and lives in Exeter, NH. He has a Bachelor of Science Degree from UNH and a Master of Science Degree from Northern Arizona University. He is a NH certified Soil Scientist and Wetland Scientist.

Reference:

Data on the atomic properties of the elements was taken from the Periodic Table created by the National Institute of Standards and Technology (NIST), U.S. Department of Commerce publication NIST SP 966 (September 2010).

Draw the Periodic Table structure.

Begin drawing the table with a block of boxes eighteen wide and four high.

There are eighteen groups of elements represented by the eighteen columns of boxes.

Add a box to the upper left corner.
This is hydrogen, an explosive gas.

Add a box to the upper right corner.
This is helium, a nonreactive noble gas.

Add four boxes to the upper left corner.
These elements have similar s electron orbitals.

Add twelve boxes to the upper right corner.
These elements have similar p electron orbitals.

To the lower right of the table add a separate block of boxes fifteen wide and two high.

These are the inner transition metals. They belong in the table where the two squares are highlighted, but are placed here to shorten the width of the table.

Atomic Number and Electron Configurations

This diagram is a conceptual model of an atom showing the electron energy levels and sublevels. Left-shaded circles represent electrons with clockwise spin; right are counter. Two electrons of opposite spin will pair to form an orbital. There is one s-orbital at the s-sublevel. There are three p-orbitals at the p-sublevel, five d-orbitals at the d-sublevel, and seven f-orbitals at the f-sublevel.

The small nucleus of the atom contains positively-charged protons with uncharged neutrons.

A neutrally charged atom will have the same number of electrons as protons (the atomic number).

Elements that have similar electron configurations will usually have similar chemical and physical properties. Notice that many of the eighteen vertical groups of elements in the table have similar electron configurations; this is what gives the table it's "periodic" nature.

s - sublevel
p - sublevel
d - sublevel
f - sublevel
Electron Energy Level
NUCLEUS

Periodic Table of The Elements

The Atomic Number is the number of protons in the atom nucleus.

Group 1	2	3	4	5	6	7	8	9	10	11	12	13	14	15	16	17	18
1 1s1																	2 1s2
3 1s2 2s1	4 1s2 2s2											5 1s2 2s2,2p1	6 1s2 2s2,2p2	7 1s2 2s2,2p3	8 1s2 2s2,2p4	9 1s2 2s2,2p5	10 1s2 2s2,2p6 Neon(Ne)
11 Ne(10) 3s1	12 Ne(10) 3s2											13 Ne(10) 3s2,3p1	14 Ne(10) 3s2,3p2	15 Ne(10) 3s2,3p3	16 Ne(10) 3s2,3p4	17 Ne(10) 3s2,3p5	18 Ne(10) 3s2,3p6 Argon(Ar)
19 Ar(18) 4s1	20 Ar(18) 4s2	21 Ar(18) 3d1 4s2	22 Ar(18) 3d2 4s2	23 Ar(18) 3d3 4s2	24 Ar(18) 3d5 4s1	25 Ar(18) 3d5 4s2	26 Ar(18) 3d6 4s2	27 Ar(18) 3d7 4s2	28 Ar(18) 3d8 4s2	29 Ar(18) 3d10 4s1	30 Ar(18) 3d10 4s2	31 Ar(18) 3d10 4s2,4p1	32 Ar(18) 3d10 4s2,4p2	33 Ar(18) 3d10 4s2,4p3	34 Ar(18) 3d10 4s2,4p4	35 Ar(18) 3d10 4s2,4p5	36 Ar(18) 3d10 4s2,4p6 Krypton(Kr)
37 Kr(36) 5s1	38 Kr(36) 5s2	39 Kr(36) 4d1 5s2	40 Kr(36) 4d2 5s2	41 Kr(36) 4d4 5s1	42 Kr(36) 4d5 5s1	43 Kr(36) 4d5 5s2	44 Kr(36) 4d7 5s1	45 Kr(36) 4d8 5s1	46 Kr(36) 4d10	47 Kr(36) 4d10 5s1	48 Kr(36) 4d10 5s2	49 Kr(36) 4d10 5s2,5p1	50 Kr(36) 4d10 5s2,5p2	51 Kr(36) 4d10 5s2,5p3	52 Kr(36) 4d10 5s2,5p4	53 Kr(36) 4d10 5s2,5p5	54 Kr(36) 4d10 5s2,5p6 Xenon(Xe)
55 Xe(54) 6s1	56 Xe(54) 6s2	57-71	72 Xe(54) 4f14 5d2 6s2	73 Xe(54) 4f14 5d3 6s2	74 Xe(54) 4f14 5d4 6s2	75 Xe(54) 4f14 5d5 6s2	76 Xe(54) 4f14 5d6 6s2	77 Xe(54) 4f14 5d7 6s2	78 Xe(54) 4f14 5d9 6s1	79 Xe(54) 4f14 5d10 6s1	80 Xe(54) 4f14 5d10 6s2	81 Xe(54) 4f14 5d10 6s2,6p1	82 Xe(54) 4f14 5d10 6s2,6p2	83 Xe(54) 4f14 5d10 6s2,6p3	84 Xe(54) 4f14 5d10 6s2,6p4	85 Xe(54) 4f14 5d10 6s2,6p5	86 Xe(54) 4f14,5d10 6s2,6p6 Radon(Rn)
87 Rn(86) 7s1	88 Rn(86) 7s2	89-103	104 Rn(86) 5f14 6d2 7s2?	105	106	107	108	109	110	111	112	113	114	115	116	117	118

Lanthanides (57–71)

57 Xe(54) 5d1 6s2	58 Xe(54) 4f1 5d1 6s2	59 Xe(54) 4f3 6s2	60 Xe(54) 4f4 6s2	61 Xe(54) 4f5 6s2	62 Xe(54) 4f6 6s2	63 Xe(54) 4f7 6s2	64 Xe(54) 4f7 5d1 6s2	65 Xe(54) 4f9 6s2	66 Xe(54) 4f10 6s2	67 Xe(54) 4f11 6s2	68 Xe(54) 4f12 6s2	69 Xe(54) 4f13 6s2	70 Xe(54) 4f14 6s2	71 Xe(54) 4f14 5d1 6s2

Actinides (89–103)

89 Rn(86) 6d1 7s2	90 Rn(86) 6d2 7s2	91 Rn(86) 5f2 6d1 7s2	92 Rn(86) 5f3 6d1 7s2	93 Rn(86) 5f4 6d1 7s2	94 Rn(86) 5f6 7s2	95 Rn(86) 5f7 7s2	96 Rn(86) 5f7 6d1 7s2	97 Rn(86) 5f9 7s2	98 Rn(86) 5f10 7s2	99 Rn(86) 5f11 7s2	100 Rn(86) 5f12 7s2	101 Rn(86) 5f13 7s2	102 Rn(86) 5f14 7s2	103 Rn(86) 5f14 7s2, 7p1?

Legend:
Electron Energy Level
Electron Sublevel
Number of Electrons
3 p 5

Ground state electron configurations are derived from the National Institute of Standards (NIST), September, 2010.

Identify groups of elements with similar chemical and physical properties.

Periodic Table of The Elements

Hydrogen — Is a non-metalic, highly combustable gas in a category of it's own.

Alkali Metals — Are highly reactive. They easily lose their outer electron to form +1 cations.

Alkaline Earth Metals — Are generally somewhat reactive. They tend to lose their outer 2 electrons to form +2 cations.

Transition Metals — Generally have incomplete d electron sublevels which can produce various magnetic properties.

Inner Transition Metals — Lanthanides and Actinides generally have incomplete f sublevels and are similar to the transition metals.

Other Metals — These metals melt at relatively low temperatures and are generally somewhat malleable.

Metalloids — Are mostly brittle solids used in making glass and electronic semi-conductors.

Nonmetals — Are the primary components of the earth's atmosphere and biosphere.

Halogens — Are highly reactive. Their nearly-complete p sublevels make them very electro-negative.

Noble Gasses — Are gasses with very low reactivity. They have full outer electron s and p sublevels.

The Atomic Number is the number of protons in the atom nucleus.

Legend:
- Alkali Metals
- Alkaline Earth Metals
- Transition Metals
- Other Metals
- Metalloids
- Nonmetals
- Halogens
- Noble Gasses

Element names and symbols are from the
National Institute of Standards (NIST), September, 2010.

5

Periodic Table of The Elements

Hydrogen and the Alkali Metals.

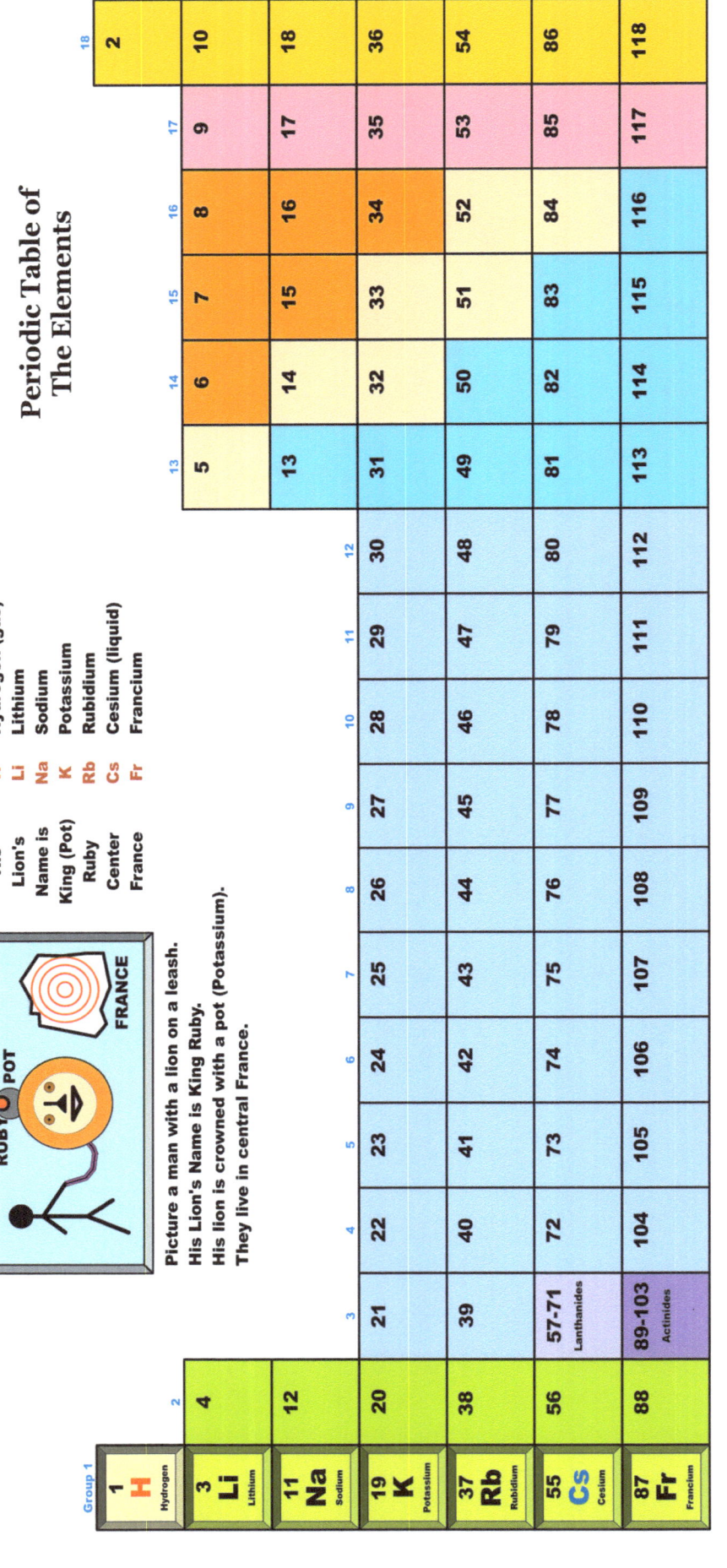

RUBY • POT

FRANCE

His
Lion's
Name is
King (Pot)
Ruby
Center
France

H	Hydrogen (gas)
Li	Lithium
Na	Sodium
K	Potassium
Rb	Rubidium
Cs	Cesium (liquid)
Fr	Francium

Picture a man with a lion on a leash.
His Lion's Name is King Ruby.
His lion is crowned with a pot (Potassium).
They live in central France.

- Alkali Metals
- Alkaline Earth Metals
- Transition Metals
- Other Metals
- Metalloids
- Nonmetals
- Halogens
- Noble Gases

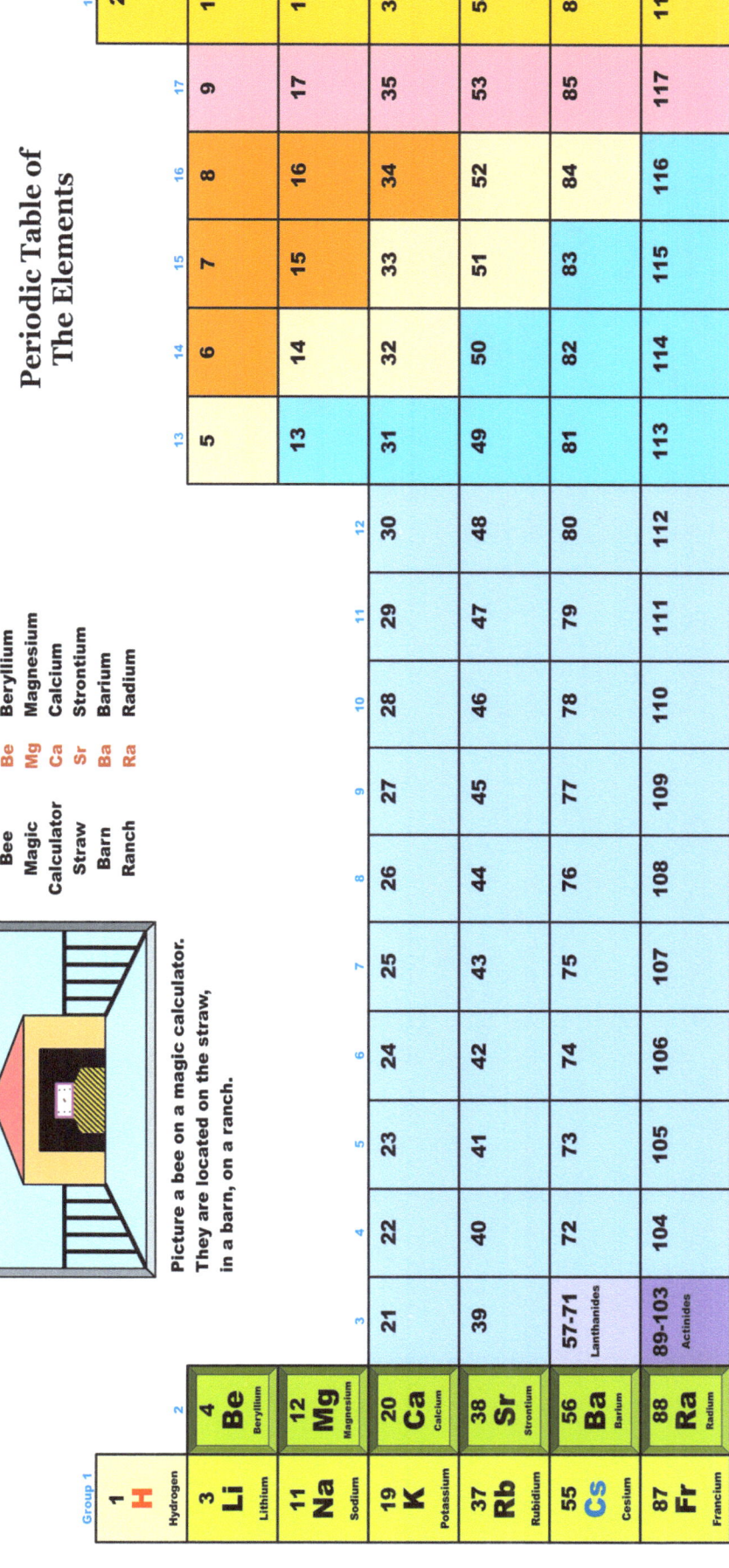

Periodic Table of The Elements

The Alkaline Earth Metals.

Bee	Be	Beryllium
Magic	Mg	Magnesium
Calculator	Ca	Calcium
Straw	Sr	Strontium
Barn	Ba	Barium
Ranch	Ra	Radium

Picture a bee on a magic calculator. They are located on the straw, in a barn, on a ranch.

Legend:
- Alkali Metals
- Alkaline Earth Metals
- Transition Metals
- Other Metals
- Metalloids
- Nonmetals
- Halogens
- Noble Gasses

The Halogens.

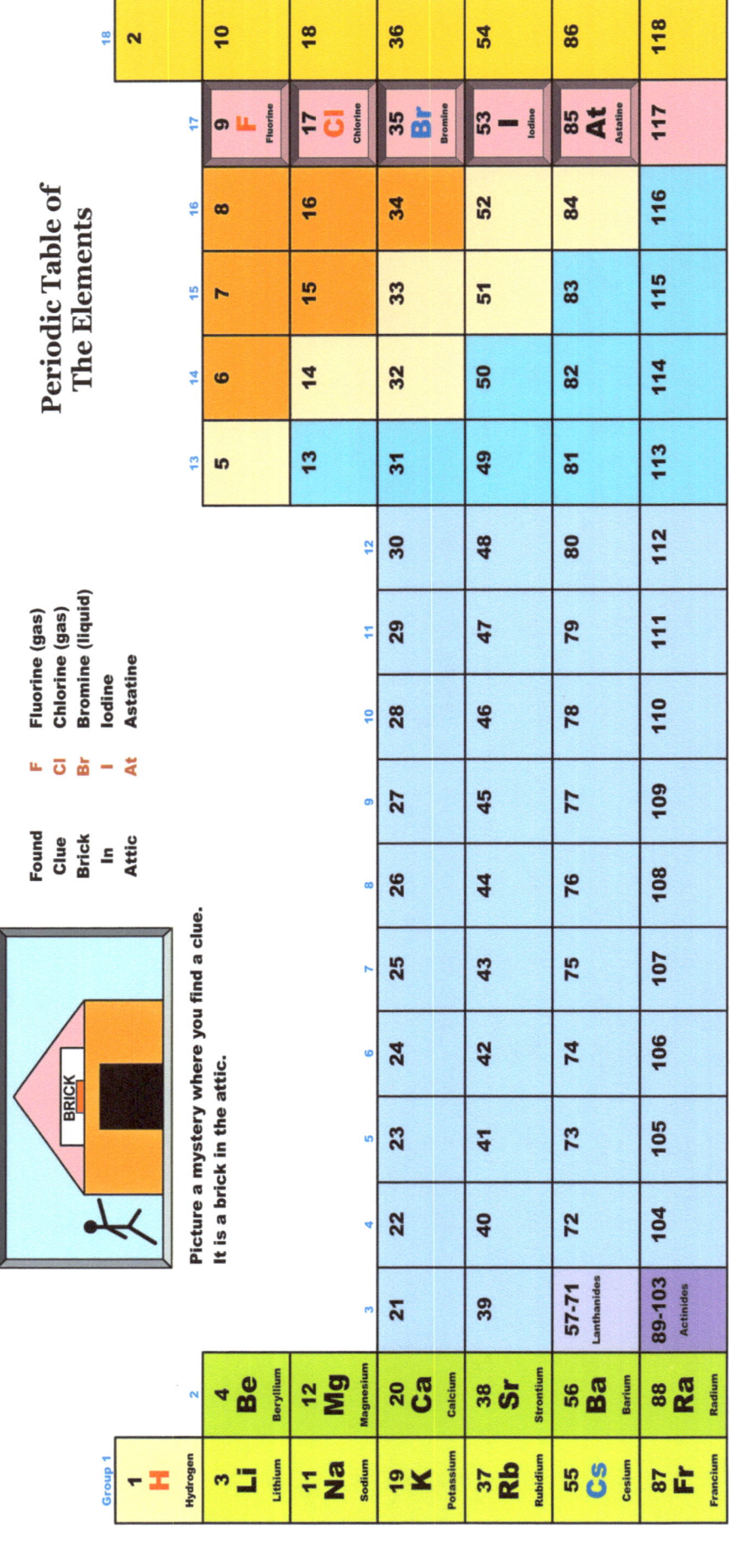

Picture a mystery where you find a clue.
It is a brick in the attic.

Found	F	Fluorine (gas)
Clue	Cl	Chlorine (gas)
Brick	Br	Bromine (liquid)
In	I	Iodine
Attic	At	Astatine

Periodic Table of
The Elements

Alkali Metals
Alkaline Earth Metals
Transition Metals
Other Metals
Metalloids
Nonmetals
Halogens
Noble Gasses

Periodic Table of The Elements

The Noble Gasses.

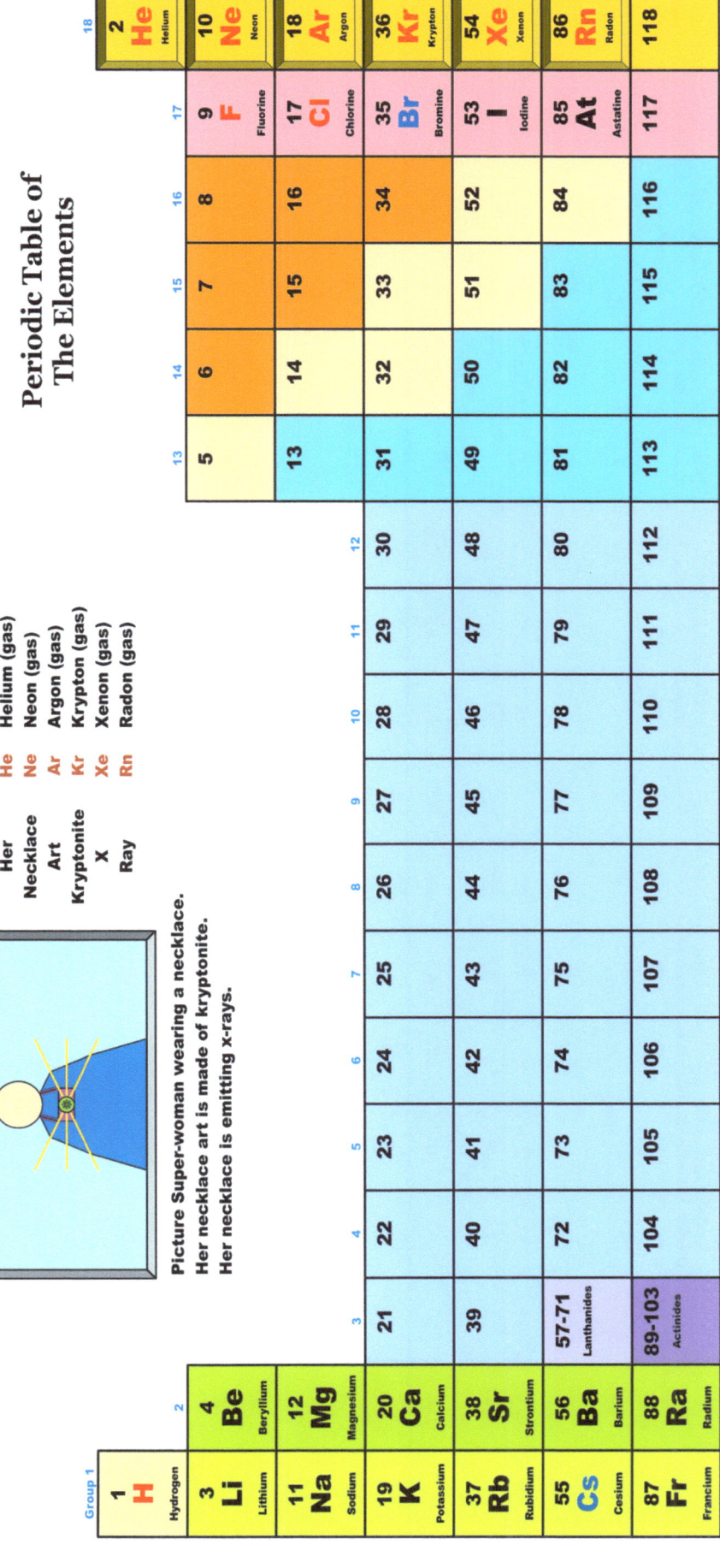

Picture Super-woman wearing a necklace.
Her necklace art is made of kryptonite.
Her necklace is emitting x-rays.

Her	He	Helium (gas)
Necklace	Ne	Neon (gas)
Art	Ar	Argon (gas)
Kryptonite	Kr	Krypton (gas)
X	Xe	Xenon (gas)
Ray	Rn	Radon (gas)

Legend:
- Alkali Metals
- Alkaline Earth Metals
- Transition Metals
- Other Metals
- Metalloids
- Nonmetals
- Halogens
- Noble Gasses

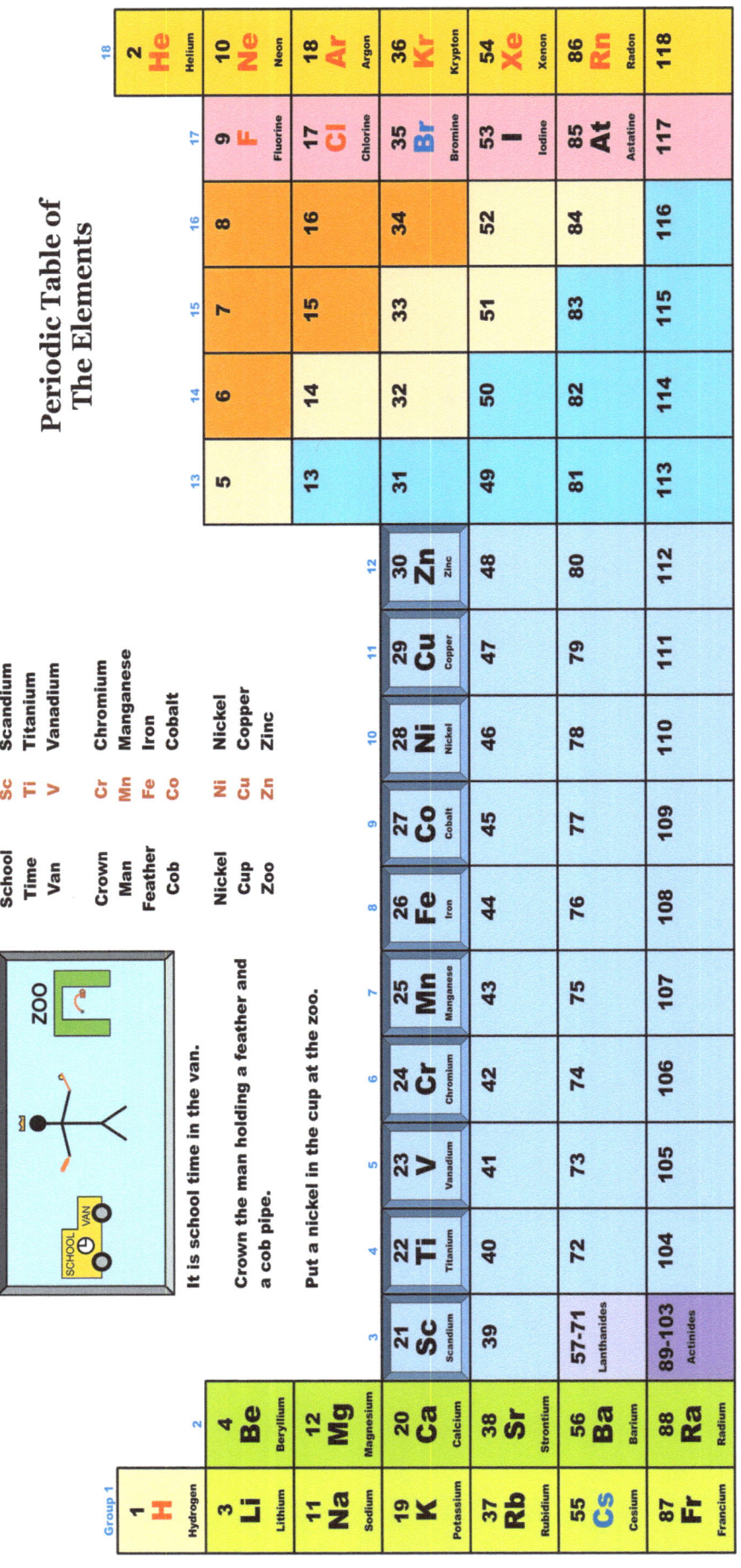

Periodic Table of The Elements

The Transition Metals.

It is school time in the van.

Crown the man holding a feather and a cob pipe.

Put a nickel in the cup at the zoo.

School	Sc	Scandium
Time	Ti	Titanium
Van	V	Vanadium
Crown	Cr	Chromium
Man	Mn	Manganese
Feather	Fe	Iron
Cob	Co	Cobalt
Nickel	Ni	Nickel
Cup	Cu	Copper
Zoo	Zn	Zinc

Legend:
- Alkali Metals
- Alkaline Earth Metals
- Transition Metals
- Other Metals
- Metalloids
- Nonmetals
- Halogens
- Noble Gasses

Group 3 and 4 Transition Metals.

Periodic Table of The Elements

School	Sc	Scandium
Year	Y	Yttrium
Lawn	La	Lanthanides
Apple	Ac	Actinides
Time	Ti	Titanium
Zero	Zr	Zirconium
Half	Hf	Hafnium
Ruff	Rf	Rutherfordium (man made)

Picture a school year calendar laying on the lawn next to an apple.

The time is zero.
Half the clock is rough textured.

Legend:
- Alkali Metals
- Alkaline Earth Metals
- Transition Metals
- Other Metals
- Metalloids
- Nonmetals
- Halogens
- Noble Gasses

Group 5 and 6 Transition Metals.

Periodic Table of The Elements

	V	Vanadium
Van	Nb	Niobium
Nibble	Ta	Tantalum
Tantalizing	Db	Dubnium (man made)
Dublin		
	Cr	Chromium
Crown	Mo	Molybdenum
Mole	W	Tungsten
White Tunic	Sg	Seaborgium (man made)
Seaboard		

Picture a person in a van nibbling tantalizing food from Dublin.

Crown the mole wearing a white tunic and sitting on the seaboard.

Legend:
- Alkali Metals
- Alkaline Earth Metals
- Transition Metals
- Other Metals
- Metalloids
- Nonmetals
- Halogens
- Noble Gasses

Group 7 and 8 Transition Metals.

Manuel is reading a technical manual.
Rheannon is a bohemian phylosopher.

The running ostritch has a feather in it.

Manuel	**Mn** Manganese
Technical	**Tc** Technetium (man-made)
Rheannon	**Re** Rhenium
Bohemian	**Bh** Bohrium (man-made)
Feather in	**Fe** Iron
Run	**Ru** Ruthenium
Ostritch	**Os** Osmium
Has	**Hs** Hassium (man-made)

Periodic Table of The Elements

Alkali Metals
Alkaline Earth Metals
Transition Metals
Other Metals
Metalloids
Nonmetals
Halogens
Noble Gasses

13

Group 9 and 10 Transition Metals.

Cob	Cobalt	Co
Rhododendron	Rhodium	Rh
Irish	Iridium	Ir
Melody	Meitnerium (man made)	Mt
Nickel	Nickel	Ni
Pallat	Palladium	Pd
Plate	Platinum	Pt
Dart	Darmstadtium (man made)	Ds

Picture a cob pipe on a rhododendron. It is playing an Irish melody.

The nickel is on a pallat, on a platinum plate, balanced on a dart.

Periodic Table of The Elements

Group 1	2	3	4	5	6	7	8	9	10	11	12	13	14	15	16	17	18
1 H Hydrogen																	2 He Helium
3 Li Lithium	4 Be Beryllium											5	6	7	8	9 F Fluorine	10 Ne Neon
11 Na Sodium	12 Mg Magnesium											13	14	15	16	17 Cl Chlorine	18 Ar Argon
19 K Potassium	20 Ca Calcium	21 Sc Scandium	22 Ti Titanium	23 V Vanadium	24 Cr Chromium	25 Mn Manganese	26 Fe Iron	27 Co Cobalt	28 Ni Nickel	29 Cu Copper	30 Zn Zinc	31	32	33	34	35 Br Bromine	36 Kr Krypton
37 Rb Rubidium	38 Sr Strontium	39 Y Yttrium	40 Zr Zirconium	41 Nb Niobium	42 Mo Molybdenum	43 Tc Technetium	44 Ru Ruthenium	45 Rh Rhodium	46 Pd Palladium	47	48	49	50	51	52	53 I Iodine	54 Xe Xenon
55 Cs Cesium	56 Ba Barium	57-71 La-Lu Lanthanides	72 Hf Hafnium	73 Ta Tantalum	74 W Tungsten	75 Re Rhenium	76 Os Osmium	77 Ir Iridium	78 Pt Platinum	79	80	81	82	83	84	85 At Astatine	86 Rn Radon
87 Fr Francium	88 Ra Radium	89-103 Ac-Lr Actinides	104 Rf Rutherfordium	105 Db Dubnium	106 Sg Seaborgium	107 Bh Bohrium	108 Hs Hassium	109 Mt Meitnerium	110 Ds Darmstadtium	111	112	113	114	115	116	117	118

57	58	59	60	61	62	63	64	65	66	67	68	69	70	71
89	90	91	92	93	94	95	96	97	98	99	100	101	102	103

- Alkali Metals
- Alkaline Earth Metals
- Transition Metals
- Other Metals
- Metalloids
- Nonmetals
- Halogens
- Noble Gasses

14

Periodic Table of The Elements

Group 11 and 12 Transition Metals.

Cup	Copper	Cu
Agronomic	Silver	Ag
Auger	Gold	Au
Rogue	Roentgenium (man made)	Rg
Zoo	Zinc	Zn
Caddie	Cadmium	Cd
Huge Merchant	Mercury (liquid)	Hg
Copenhagen	Copernicium (man made)	Cn

Copenhagen Zoo

Dig for copper, silver and gold coins with an agronomic auger, you rogue.

The golf zoo in Copenhagen has a caddie for a huge merchant.

Group 1: 1 H Hydrogen, 3 Li Lithium, 11 Na Sodium, 19 K Potassium, 37 Rb Rubidium, 55 Cs Cesium, 87 Fr Francium

Group 2: 4 Be Beryllium, 12 Mg Magnesium, 20 Ca Calcium, 38 Sr Strontium, 56 Ba Barium, 88 Ra Radium

Group 3: 21 Sc Scandium, 39 Y Yttrium, 57-71 La-Lu Lanthanides, 89-103 Ac-Lr Actinides

Group 4: 22 Ti Titanium, 40 Zr Zirconium, 72 Hf Hafnium, 104 Rf Rutherfordium

Group 5: 23 V Vanadium, 41 Nb Niobium, 73 Ta Tantalum, 105 Db Dubnium

Group 6: 24 Cr Chromium, 42 Mo Molybdenum, 74 W Tungsten, 106 Sg Seaborgium

Group 7: 25 Mn Manganese, 43 Tc Technetium, 75 Re Rhenium, 107 Bh Bohrium

Group 8: 26 Fe Iron, 44 Ru Ruthenium, 76 Os Osmium, 108 Hs Hassium

Group 9: 27 Co Cobalt, 45 Rh Rhodium, 77 Ir Iridium, 109 Mt Meitnerium

Group 10: 28 Ni Nickel, 46 Pd Palladium, 78 Pt Platinum, 110 Ds Darmstadtium

Group 11: 29 Cu Copper, 47 Ag Silver, 79 Au Gold, 111 Rg Roentgenium

Group 12: 30 Zn Zinc, 48 Cd Cadmium, 80 Hg Mercury, 112 Cn Copernicium

Group 13: 5, 13, 31, 49, 81, 113

Group 14: 6, 14, 32, 50, 82, 114

Group 15: 7, 15, 33, 51, 83, 115

Group 16: 8, 16, 34, 52, 84, 116

Group 17: 9 F Fluorine, 17 Cl Chlorine, 35 Br Bromine, 53 I Iodine, 85 At Astatine, 117

Group 18: 2 He Helium, 10 Ne Neon, 18 Ar Argon, 36 Kr Krypton, 54 Xe Xenon, 86 Rn Radon, 118

Lanthanides: 57, 58, 59, 60, 61, 62, 63, 64, 65, 66, 67, 68, 69, 70, 71

Actinides: 89, 90, 91, 92, 93, 94, 95, 96, 97, 98, 99, 100, 101, 102, 103

Legend:
- Alkali Metals
- Alkaline Earth Metals
- Transition Metals
- Other Metals
- Metalloids
- Nonmetals
- Halogens
- Noble Gasses

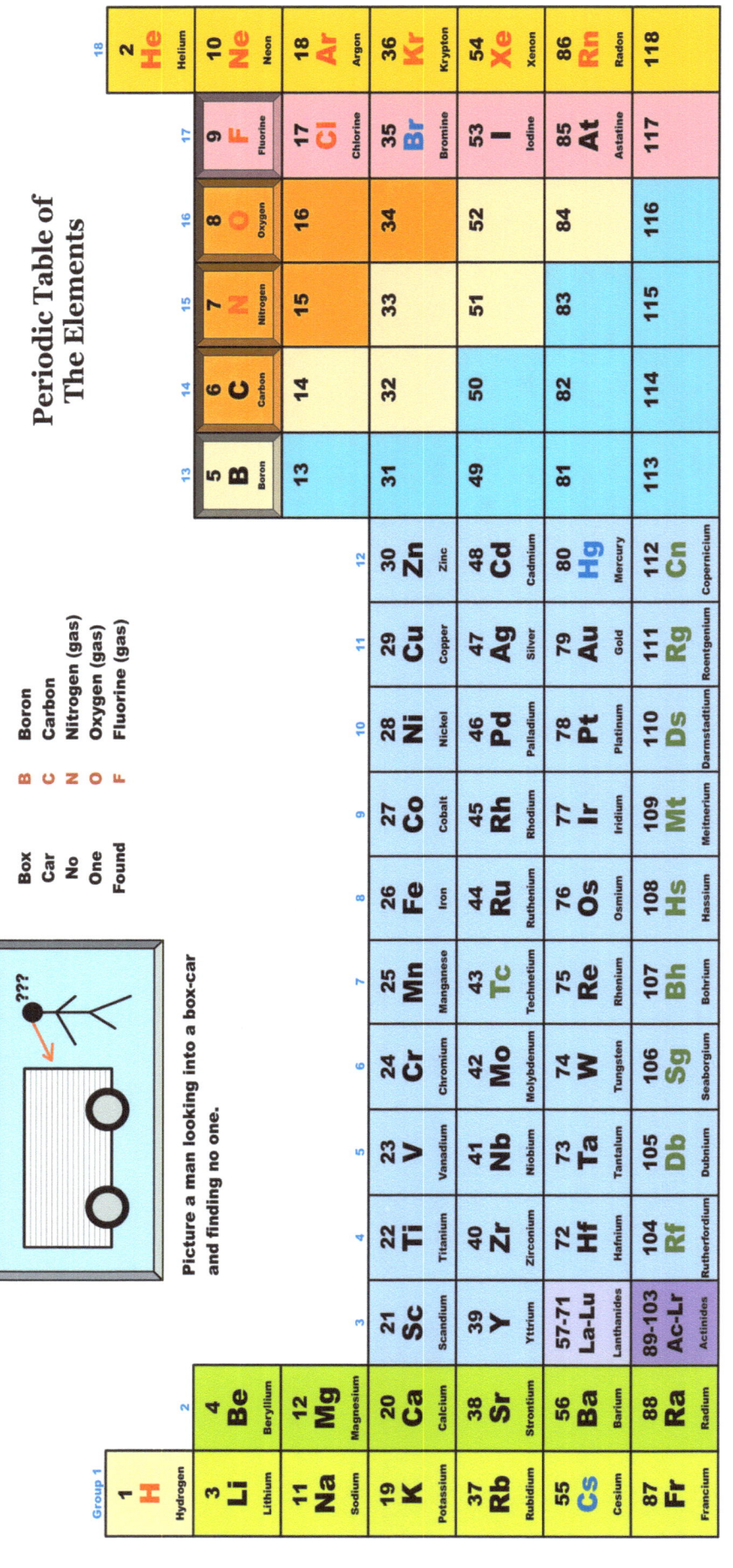

Periodic Table of The Elements

The p-Block Elements.

Picture a man looking into a box-car and finding no one.

Box	Car	No	One	Found
Boron	Carbon	Nitrogen (gas)	Oxygen (gas)	Fluorine (gas)
B	C	N	O	F

Legend:
- Alkali Metals
- Alkaline Earth Metals
- Transition Metals
- Other Metals
- Metalloids
- Nonmetals
- Halogens
- Noble Gasses

Periodic Table of The Elements

Group 13 and 14 Elements.

BOX ALL GALLONS | CAR SIGNAL | TINS OF PLUMS

IN THAT

GERMAN

Box all gallons in that.

Car signal on the german car.
Tins of plums on the car.

| Box | All | Gallons | In | That | Boron | Aluminum | Gallium (liquid) | Indium | Thallium |
| Car | Signal | German | TinS | PLum | Carbon | Silicon | Germanium | Tin | Lead |

| B | Al | Ga | In | Tl | Boron | Aluminum | Gallium | Indium | Thallium |
| C | Si | Ge | Sn | Pb | Carbon | Silicon | Germanium | Tin | Lead |

Group 1																	18
1 H Hydrogen	2											13	14	15	16	17	2 He Helium
3 Li Lithium	4 Be Beryllium											5 B Boron	6 C Carbon	7 N Nitrogen	8 O Oxygen	9 F Fluorine	10 Ne Neon
11 Na Sodium	12 Mg Magnesium	3	4	5	6	7	8	9	10	11	12	13 Al Aluminum	14 Si Silicon	15	16	17 Cl Chlorine	18 Ar Argon
19 K Potassium	20 Ca Calcium	21 Sc Scandium	22 Ti Titanium	23 V Vanadium	24 Cr Chromium	25 Mn Manganese	26 Fe Iron	27 Co Cobalt	28 Ni Nickel	29 Cu Copper	30 Zn Zinc	31 Ga Gallium	32 Ge Germanium	33	34	35 Br Bromine	36 Kr Krypton
37 Rb Rubidium	38 Sr Strontium	39 Y Yttrium	40 Zr Zirconium	41 Nb Niobium	42 Mo Molybdenum	43 Tc Technetium	44 Ru Ruthenium	45 Rh Rhodium	46 Pd Palladium	47 Ag Silver	48 Cd Cadmium	49 In Indium	50 Sn Tin	51	52	53 I Iodine	54 Xe Xenon
55 Cs Cesium	56 Ba Barium	57-71 La-Lu Lanthanides	72 Hf Hafnium	73 Ta Tantalum	74 W Tungsten	75 Re Rhenium	76 Os Osmium	77 Ir Iridium	78 Pt Platinum	79 Au Gold	80 Hg Mercury	81 Tl Thallium	82 Pb Lead	83	84	85 At Astatine	86 Rn Radon
87 Fr Francium	88 Ra Radium	89-103 Ac-Lr Actinides	104 Rf Rutherfordium	105 Db Dubnium	106 Sg Seaborgium	107 Bh Bohrium	108 Hs Hassium	109 Mt Meitnerium	110 Ds Darmstadtium	111 Rg Roentgenium	112 Cn Copernicium	113	114	115	116	117	118

57	58	59	60	61	62	63	64	65	66	67	68	69	70	71
89	90	91	92	93	94	95	96	97	98	99	100	101	102	103

- Alkali Metals
- Alkaline Earth Metals
- Transition Metals
- Other Metals
- Metalloids
- Nonmetals
- Halogens
- Noble Gasses

17

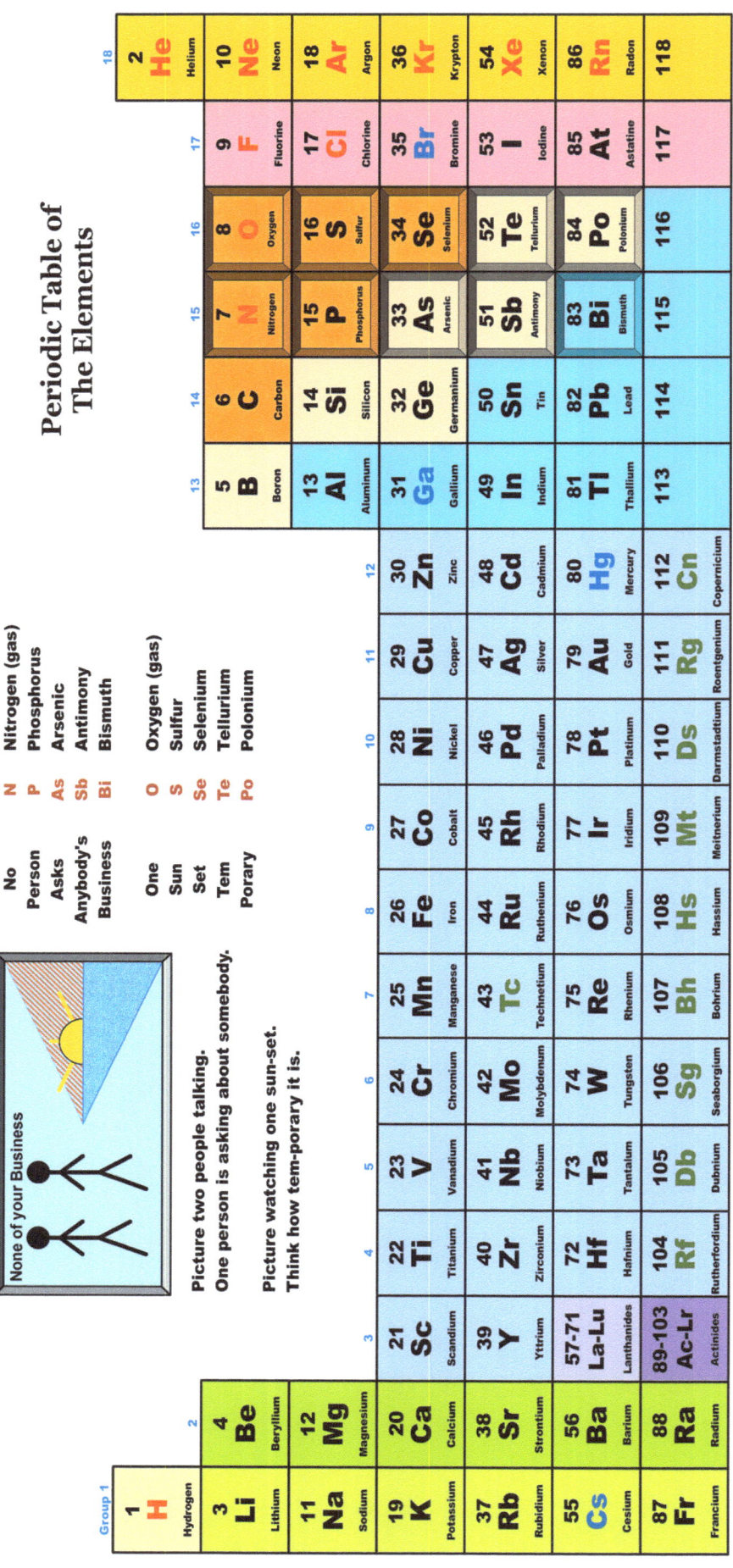

Periodic Table of The Elements

Group 15 and 16 Elements.

None of your Business

Picture two people talking.
One person is asking about somebody.

Picture watching one sun-set.
Think how tem-porary it is.

No	N	Nitrogen (gas)
Person	P	Phosphorus
Asks	As	Arsenic
Anybody's	Sb	Antimony
Business	Bi	Bismuth
One	O	Oxygen (gas)
Sun	S	Sulfur
Set	Se	Selenium
Tem	Te	Tellurium
Porary	Po	Polonium

Legend:
- ☐ Alkali Metals
- ☐ Alkaline Earth Metals
- ☐ Transition Metals
- ☐ Other Metals
- ☐ Metalloids
- ☐ Nonmetals
- ☐ Halogens
- ☐ Noble Gasses

Periodic Table of The Elements

New Unnamed Man Made Elements.

Quiet

Picture the quiet person in a library.
She has some oranges.

Uut	Ununtrium (man made)
Uuq	Ununquadium (man made)
Uup	Ununpentium (man made)
Uuh	Ununhexium (man made)
Uus	Ununseptium (man made)
Uuo	Ununoctium (man made)

The
Quiet
Person
Has
Some
Oranges

Legend:
- Alkali Metals
- Alkaline Earth Metals
- Transition Metals
- Other Metals
- Metalloids
- Nonmetals
- Halogens
- Noble Gasses

19

Periodic Table of The Elements

The Lanthanide Inner-Transition Metals.

| Lantern | Gadget Makes | Thumb in |
| Ceremony | Terrible Dye | Yearbook |

Lute

Hole in Herb

Praise Prom (Sam)
Neon Europe

Picture a lantern ceremony.
Praise the neon.
Sam went to the prom in Europe.

A gadget makes a terrible dye.
The dye makes a hole in the herb.
A thumb is in the yearbook.
There is a picture of a lute.

Lantern	La	Lanthanum
Ceremony	Ce	Cerium
Praise	Pr	Praseodymium
Neon	Nd	Neodymium
Prom	Pm	Promethium (man made)
Sam	Sm	Samarium
Europe	Eu	Europium
Gadget	Gd	Gadolinium
Terrible	Tb	Terbium
Dye	Dy	Dysprosium
Hole	Ho	Holmium
Herb	Er	Erbium
Thumb	Tm	Thulium
Yearbook	Yb	Ytterbium
Lute	Lu	Lutetium

Legend
- Alkali Metals
- Alkaline Earth Metals
- Transition Metals
- Other Metals
- Metalloids
- Nonmetals
- Halogens
- Noble Gasses

Periodic table (element symbols)

Group 1: 1 H Hydrogen; 3 Li Lithium; 11 Na Sodium; 19 K Potassium; 37 Rb Rubidium; 55 Cs Cesium; 87 Fr Francium

Group 2: 4 Be Beryllium; 12 Mg Magnesium; 20 Ca Calcium; 38 Sr Strontium; 56 Ba Barium; 88 Ra Radium

Group 3: 21 Sc Scandium; 39 Y Yttrium; 57-71 La-Lu Lanthanides; 89-103 Ac-Lr Actinides

Group 4: 22 Ti Titanium; 40 Zr Zirconium; 72 Hf Hafnium; 104 Rf Rutherfordium

Group 5: 23 V Vanadium; 41 Nb Niobium; 73 Ta Tantalum; 105 Db Dubnium

Group 6: 24 Cr Chromium; 42 Mo Molybdenum; 74 W Tungsten; 106 Sg Seaborgium

Group 7: 25 Mn Manganese; 43 Tc Technetium; 75 Re Rhenium; 107 Bh Bohrium

Group 8: 26 Fe Iron; 44 Ru Ruthenium; 76 Os Osmium; 108 Hs Hassium

Group 9: 27 Co Cobalt; 45 Rh Rhodium; 77 Ir Iridium; 109 Mt Meitnerium

Group 10: 28 Ni Nickel; 46 Pd Palladium; 78 Pt Platinum; 110 Ds Darmstadtium

Group 11: 29 Cu Copper; 47 Ag Silver; 79 Au Gold; 111 Rg Roentgenium

Group 12: 30 Zn Zinc; 48 Cd Cadmium; 80 Hg Mercury; 112 Cn Copernicium

Group 13: 5 B Boron; 13 Al Aluminum; 31 Ga Gallium; 49 In Indium; 81 Tl Thallium; 113 Uut Ununtrium

Group 14: 6 C Carbon; 14 Si Silicon; 32 Ge Germanium; 50 Sn Tin; 82 Pb Lead; 114 Uuq Ununquadium

Group 15: 7 N Nitrogen; 15 P Phosphorus; 33 As Arsenic; 51 Sb Antimony; 83 Bi Bismuth; 115 Uup Ununpentium

Group 16: 8 O Oxygen; 16 S Sulfur; 34 Se Selenium; 52 Te Tellurium; 84 Po Polonium; 116 Uuh Ununhexium

Group 17: 9 F Fluorine; 17 Cl Chlorine; 35 Br Bromine; 53 I Iodine; 85 At Astatine; 117 Uus Ununseptium

Group 18: 2 He Helium; 10 Ne Neon; 18 Ar Argon; 36 Kr Krypton; 54 Xe Xenon; 86 Rn Radon; 118 Uuo Ununoctium

Lanthanides row: 57 La Lanthanum; 58 Ce Cerium; 59 Pr Praseodymium; 60 Nd Neodymium; 61 Pm Promethium; 62 Sm Samarium; 63 Eu Europium; 64 Gd Gadolinium; 65 Tb Terbium; 66 Dy Dysprosium; 67 Ho Holmium; 68 Er Erbium; 69 Tm Thulium; 70 Yb Ytterbium; 71 Lu Lutetium

Actinides row: 89; 90; 91; 92; 93; 94; 95; 96; 97; 98; 99; 100; 101; 102; 103

The Actinide Inner-Transition Metals.

Periodic Table of The Elements

Picture an actor who gets thirsty. She is protected under nice pines.

An American cure in Berkeley California.

Einstein uses a fern to mend the nobel law.

Mnemonic	Symbol	Element
Actor	Ac	Actinium
Thirsty	Th	Thorium
Protected	Pa	Protactinium
Under	U	Uranium
Nice	Np	Neptunium (man made)
Pines	Pu	Plutonium (man made)
American	Am	Americium (man made)
Cure	Cm	Curium (man made)
Berkeley	Bk	Berkelium (man made)
California	Cf	Californium (man made)
Einstein	Es	Einsteinium (man made)
Fern	Fm	Fermium (man made)
Mend	Md	Mendelevium (man made)
Nobel	No	Nobelium (man made)
Law	Lr	Lawrencium (man made)

Group 1	2	3	4	5	6	7	8	9	10	11	12	13	14	15	16	17	18
1 H Hydrogen																	2 He Helium
3 Li Lithium	4 Be Beryllium											5 B Boron	6 C Carbon	7 N Nitrogen	8 O Oxygen	9 F Fluorine	10 Ne Neon
11 Na Sodium	12 Mg Magnesium											13 Al Aluminum	14 Si Silicon	15 P Phosphorus	16 S Sulfur	17 Cl Chlorine	18 Ar Argon
19 K Potassium	20 Ca Calcium	21 Sc Scandium	22 Ti Titanium	23 V Vanadium	24 Cr Chromium	25 Mn Manganese	26 Fe Iron	27 Co Cobalt	28 Ni Nickel	29 Cu Copper	30 Zn Zinc	31 Ga Gallium	32 Ge Germanium	33 As Arsenic	34 Se Selenium	35 Br Bromine	36 Kr Krypton
37 Rb Rubidium	38 Sr Strontium	39 Y Yttrium	40 Zr Zirconium	41 Nb Niobium	42 Mo Molybdenum	43 Tc Technetium	44 Ru Ruthenium	45 Rh Rhodium	46 Pd Palladium	47 Ag Silver	48 Cd Cadmium	49 In Indium	50 Sn Tin	51 Sb Antimony	52 Te Tellurium	53 I Iodine	54 Xe Xenon
55 Cs Cesium	56 Ba Barium	57-71 La-Lu Lanthanides	72 Hf Hafnium	73 Ta Tantalum	74 W Tungsten	75 Re Rhenium	76 Os Osmium	77 Ir Iridium	78 Pt Platinum	79 Au Gold	80 Hg Mercury	81 Tl Thallium	82 Pb Lead	83 Bi Bismuth	84 Po Polonium	85 At Astatine	86 Rn Radon
87 Fr Francium	88 Ra Radium	89-103 Ac-Lr Actinides	104 Rf Rutherfordium	105 Db Dubnium	106 Sg Seaborgium	107 Bh Bohrium	108 Hs Hassium	109 Mt Meitnerium	110 Ds Darmstadtium	111 Rg Roentgenium	112 Cn Copernicium	113 Uut Ununtrium	114 Uuq Ununquadium	115 Uup Ununpentium	116 Uuh Ununhexium	117 Uus Ununseptium	118 Uuo Ununoctium

57 La Lanthanum	58 Ce Cerium	59 Pr Praseodymium	60 Nd Neodymium	61 Pm Promethium	62 Sm Samarium	63 Eu Europium	64 Gd Gadolinium	65 Tb Terbium	66 Dy Dysprosium	67 Ho Holmium	68 Er Erbium	69 Tm Thulium	70 Yb Ytterbium	71 Lu Lutetium
89 Ac Actinium	90 Th Thorium	91 Pa Protactinium	92 U Uranium	93 Np Neptunium	94 Pu Plutonium	95 Am Americium	96 Cm Curium	97 Bk Berkelium	98 Cf Californium	99 Es Einsteinium	100 Fm Fermium	101 Md Mendelevium	102 No Nobelium	103 Lr Lawrencium

Legend:
- Alkali Metals
- Alkaline Earth Metals
- Transition Metals
- Other Metals
- Metalloids
- Nonmetals
- Halogens
- Noble Gasses

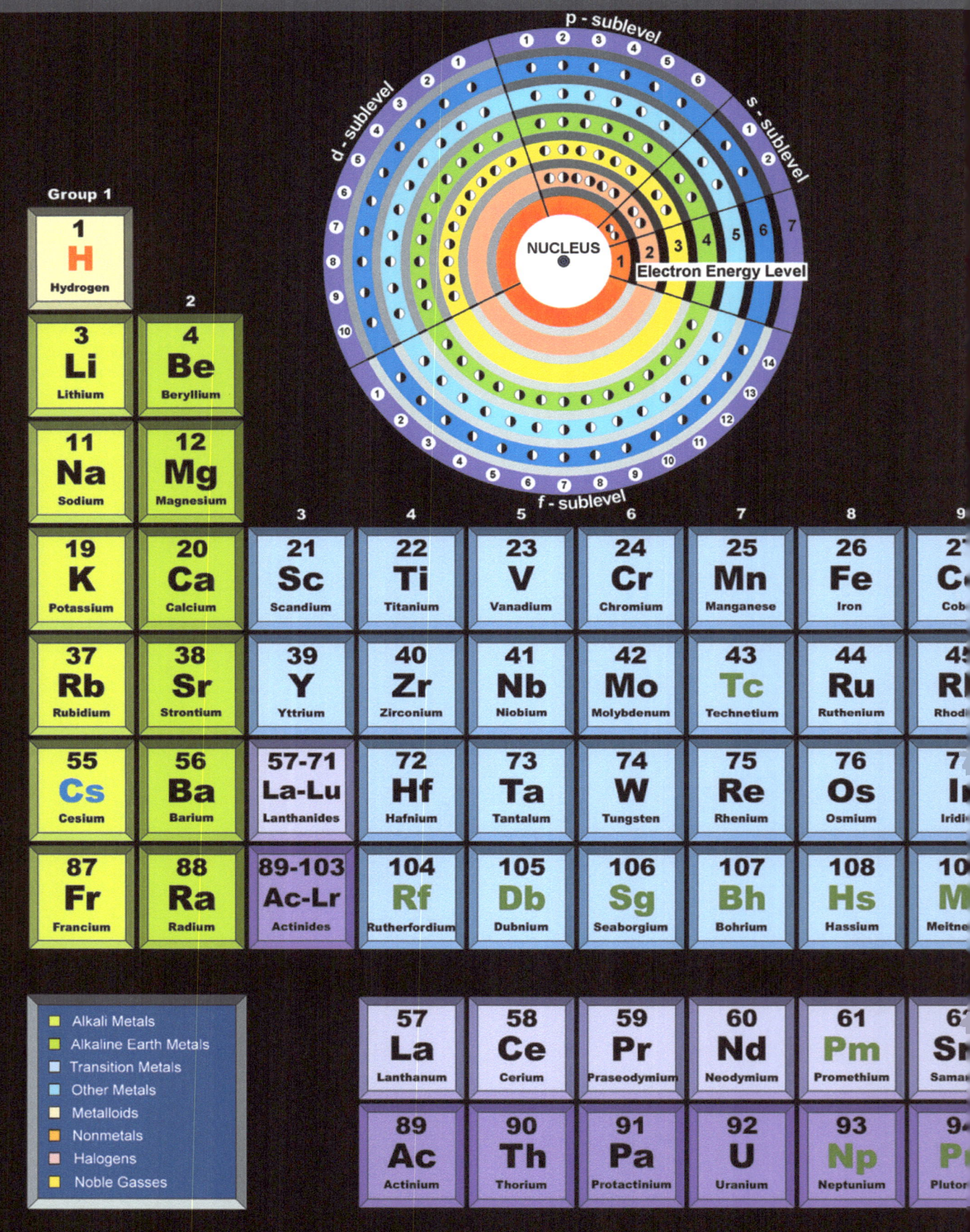

Group 1

1 **H** Hydrogen	

3 **Li** Lithium	**4** **Be** Beryllium	2
11 **Na** Sodium	**12** **Mg** Magnesium	

p - sublevel

s - sublevel

d - sublevel

NUCLEUS

Electron Energy Level

f - sublevel

3	4	5	6	7	8	9
21 **Sc** Scandium	**22** **Ti** Titanium	**23** **V** Vanadium	**24** **Cr** Chromium	**25** **Mn** Manganese	**26** **Fe** Iron	**2?** **C** Cob

19 **K** Potassium	**20** **Ca** Calcium
37 **Rb** Rubidium	**38** **Sr** Strontium
55 **Cs** Cesium	**56** **Ba** Barium
87 **Fr** Francium	**88** **Ra** Radium

39 **Y** Yttrium	**40** **Zr** Zirconium	**41** **Nb** Niobium	**42** **Mo** Molybdenum	**43** **Tc** Technetium	**44** **Ru** Ruthenium	**45** **R?** Rhodi
57-71 **La-Lu** Lanthanides	**72** **Hf** Hafnium	**73** **Ta** Tantalum	**74** **W** Tungsten	**75** **Re** Rhenium	**76** **Os** Osmium	**7?** **I?** Iridi?
89-103 **Ac-Lr** Actinides	**104** **Rf** Rutherfordium	**105** **Db** Dubnium	**106** **Sg** Seaborgium	**107** **Bh** Bohrium	**108** **Hs** Hassium	**10?** **M?** Meitne?

- 🟩 Alkali Metals
- 🟢 Alkaline Earth Metals
- ⬜ Transition Metals
- 🟦 Other Metals
- ⬜ Metalloids
- 🟧 Nonmetals
- 🟧 Halogens
- 🟨 Noble Gasses

57 **La** Lanthanum	**58** **Ce** Cerium	**59** **Pr** Praseodymium	**60** **Nd** Neodymium	**61** **Pm** Promethium	**6?** **S?** Sama?
89 **Ac** Actinium	**90** **Th** Thorium	**91** **Pa** Protactinium	**92** **U** Uranium	**93** **Np** Neptunium	**9?** **P?** Pluton?

Periodic Table of
The Elements

						18
						2 **He** Helium
13	14	15	16	17		
5 **B** Boron	**6** **C** Carbon	**7** **N** Nitrogen	**8** **O** Oxygen	**9** **F** Fluorine		**10** **Ne** Neon
13 **Al** Aluminum	**14** **Si** Silicon	**15** **P** Phosphorus	**16** **S** Sulfur	**17** **Cl** Chlorine		**18** **Ar** Argon

10	11	12						
28 **Ni** Nickel	**29** **Cu** Copper	**30** **Zn** Zinc	**31** **Ga** Gallium	**32** **Ge** Germanium	**33** **As** Arsenic	**34** **Se** Selenium	**35** **Br** Bromine	**36** **Kr** Krypton
46 **Pd** Palladium	**47** **Ag** Silver	**48** **Cd** Cadmium	**49** **In** Indium	**50** **Sn** Tin	**51** **Sb** Antimony	**52** **Te** Tellurium	**53** **I** Iodine	**54** **Xe** Xenon
78 **Pt** Platinum	**79** **Au** Gold	**80** **Hg** Mercury	**81** **Tl** Thallium	**82** **Pb** Lead	**83** **Bi** Bismuth	**84** **Po** Polonium	**85** **At** Astatine	**86** **Rn** Radon
110 **Ds** Darmstadtium	**111** **Rg** Roentgenium	**112** **Cn** Copernicium	**113** **Uut** Ununtrium	**114** **Uuq** Ununquadium	**115** **Uup** Ununpentium	**116** **Uuh** Ununhexium	**117** **Uus** Ununseptium	**118** **Uuo** Ununoctium

63 **Eu** Europium	**64** **Gd** Gadolinium	**65** **Tb** Terbium	**66** **Dy** Dysprosium	**67** **Ho** Holmium	**68** **Er** Erbium	**69** **Tm** Thulium	**70** **Yb** Ytterbium	**71** **Lu** Lutetium
95 **Am** Americium	**96** **Cm** Curium	**97** **Bk** Berkelium	**98** **Cf** Californium	**99** **Es** Einsteinium	**100** **Fm** Fermium	**101** **Md** Mendelevium	**102** **No** Nobelium	**103** **Lr** Lawrencium

Subatomic Particles and Atomic Weight.

All things on earth are made up of combinations of the elements in this table.

Each atom of these elements is made up of protons, electrons and neutrons.

Protons and electrons have equal and opposite charges (positive and negative respectivly), while neutrons have no charge.

Protons and neutrons have nearly equal mass while electrons have a mass about 1/1840 that of a proton.

An atomic mass unit (amu) is defined as 1/12 the mass of a carbon-12 atom and is approximately the mass of a proton. A carbon-12 atom consists of 6 protons, 6 neutrons and 6 electrons.

Most elements have more than one isotope. Approximately 1.07 percent of all carbon atoms contain 7 neutrons and are the carbon-13 isotope of carbon, which has slightly more mass than a carbon-12 atom. The weighted average mass of carbon-12 and carbon-13 isotopes is 12.011 amu and is the atomic weight.

The atomic weight of an element is the weighted average mass of the isotopes of that element. The atomic weight (rounded to three decimals) is labeled below the element's name.*

Periodic Table of The Elements

Group 1	2	3	4	5	6	7	8	9	10	11	12	13	14	15	16	17	18
1 H Hydrogen 1.008																	2 He Helium 4.003
3 Li Lithium 6.941	4 Be Beryllium 9.012											5 B Boron 10.811	6 C Carbon 12.011	7 N Nitrogen 14.007	8 O Oxygen 15.999	9 F Fluorine 18.998	10 Ne Neon 20.180
11 Na Sodium 22.990	12 Mg Magnesium 24.305											13 Al Aluminum 26.982	14 Si Silicon 28.086	15 P Phosphorus 30.974	16 S Sulfur 32.065	17 Cl Chlorine 35.453	18 Ar Argon 39.948
19 K Potassium 39.098	20 Ca Calcium 40.078	21 Sc Scandium 44.956	22 Ti Titanium 47.867	23 V Vanadium 50.942	24 Cr Chromium 51.996	25 Mn Manganese 54.938	26 Fe Iron 55.845	27 Co Cobalt 58.933	28 Ni Nickel 58.693	29 Cu Copper 63.546	30 Zn Zinc 65.38	31 Ga Gallium 69.723	32 Ge Germanium 72.64	33 As Arsenic 74.922	34 Se Selenium 78.96	35 Br Bromine 79.904	36 Kr Krypton 83.798
37 Rb Rubidium 85.468	38 Sr Strontium 87.62	39 Y Yttrium 88.906	40 Zr Zirconium 91.224	41 Nb Niobium 92.906	42 Mo Molybdenum 95.96	43 Tc Technetium (98)	44 Ru Ruthenium 101.07	45 Rh Rhodium 102.906	46 Pd Palladium 106.42	47 Ag Silver 107.868	48 Cd Cadmium 112.411	49 In Indium 114.818	50 Sn Tin 118.710	51 Sb Antimony 121.760	52 Te Tellurium 127.60	53 I Iodine 126.904	54 Xe Xenon 131.293
55 Cs Cesium 132.905	56 Ba Barium 137.327	57-71 La-Lu Lanthanides	72 Hf Hafnium 178.49	73 Ta Tantalum 180.948	74 W Tungsten 183.84	75 Re Rhenium 186.207	76 Os Osmium 190.23	77 Ir Iridium 192.217	78 Pt Platinum 195.084	79 Au Gold 196.967	80 Hg Mercury 200.59	81 Tl Thallium 204.383	82 Pb Lead 207.2	83 Bi Bismuth 208.980	84 Po Polonium (209)	85 At Astatine (210)	86 Rn Radon (222)
87 Fr Francium (223)	88 Ra Radium (226)	89-103 Ac-Lr Actinides	104 Rf Rutherfordium (265)	105 Db Dubnium (268)	106 Sg Seaborgium (271)	107 Bh Bohrium (272)	108 Hs Hassium (277)	109 Mt Meitnerium (276)	110 Ds Darmstadtium (281)	111 Rg Roentgenium (280)	112 Cn Copernicium (285)	113 Uut Ununtrium (284)	114 Uuq Ununquadium (289)	115 Uup Ununpentium (288)	116 Uuh Ununhexium (293)	117 Uus Ununseptium (294)	118 Uuo Ununoctium (294)

57 La Lanthanum 138.905	58 Ce Cerium 140.116	59 Pr Praseodymium 140.908	60 Nd Neodymium 144.242	61 Pm Promethium (145)	62 Sm Samarium 150.36	63 Eu Europium 151.964	64 Gd Gadolinium 157.25	65 Tb Terbium 158.925	66 Dy Dysprosium 162.500	67 Ho Holmium 164.930	68 Er Erbium 167.259	69 Tm Thulium 168.934	70 Yb Ytterbium 173.054	71 Lu Lutetium 174.967
89 Ac Actinium (227)	90 Th Thorium 232.038	91 Pa Protactinium 231.036	92 U Uranium 238.029	93 Np Neptunium (237)	94 Pu Plutonium (244)	95 Am Americium (243)	96 Cm Curium (247)	97 Bk Berkelium (247)	98 Cf Californium (251)	99 Es Einsteinium (252)	100 Fm Fermium (257)	101 Md Mendelevium (258)	102 No Nobelium (259)	103 Lr Lawrencium (262)

□ Alkali Metals
□ Alkaline Earth Metals
□ Transition Metals
□ Other Metals
□ Metalloids
□ Nonmetals
□ Halogens
□ Noble Gases

* Atomic weight derived from the National Institute of Standards (NIST), September, 2010.
( ) indicates the atomic mass number of the longest-lived isotope.

24